I'M A MANAGER

*A practical **guide to success** as
a **first time** people manager
in **professional** services.*

I'M A MANAGER

*A practical **guide to success** as a **first time** people manager in **professional** services.*

By Sue Willcock

MBA Construction & Real Estate, Dip Proj Man (RICS) Assoc CIPD, NLP Certified Practitioner

Published by Chaseville Press

First Edition: 2016

ISBN 978-0-9935247-0-7

Dedication

For Philip Youell

A man who completely changed my career through trust, encouragement and support, along with a big fat dose of fun and laughter.

Thank you.

Table of Contents

Preface

When I was first given a management role in a property and construction consultancy (ranked in the top 5 in the UK at the time), I went home with mixed emotions - proud at having been promoted, but with brow furrowed. I was excited that someone trusted me with their team and that I had new responsibilities and a challenge ahead, but was also concerned that I didn't have the skills and experience I needed to make a success of my new role.

How on earth was *I* going to manage a team?

I had trained and qualified as a Chartered Surveyor (MRICS) but had always got more satisfaction at work from the people and non-technical side of the job.

When I look back on my trainee days, I was often the person sent to speak to anyone who was being a bit grumpy on a project, to ask for more information or get them to talk things over. I like dealing with people and I like to talk. So, in many ways, leading and managing others was really exciting for me.

But, some of my team had lot more experience than I did. Despite having just finished an MBA (in Construction & Real Estate, so very specific to my sector), I had scant experience of actually sitting in front of people and running a decent meeting (let alone an inspirational one) or sitting down with someone individually and appraising them.

I did have some great mentors, both at work (one who went on to be the CEO at EC Harris LLP, now Arcadis) and at home (a good friend who was a Partner at Davis Langdon, now Aecom). So I was, in essence, surrounded by people worth listening to.

So, I listened and I'll admit, sometimes I literally just did what they told me to do.

And most of the time, it worked. Sometimes though, I just had to make stuff up as I went along.

Like many new managers before me, I did not have a live hotline to an experienced and brilliant manager when I was sitting opposite someone in room on my own, when they had suffered a loss in their family, or when they needed to be supported on a road to improving poor performance. Or they wanted to leave. Or were caught doing something they shouldn't. Or needed support through their exams. Or when they wanted to just shout at someone and I was the nearest person. Or when I had messed up and all I really needed to do was apologise.

It was a challenging transition and I do not stand before you as a perfect manager.

But, by listening, trusting, 'being brave' and applying what I learned from others and from my mistakes (some of them cringe-worthy), I did get my first team working well together and producing results.

I progressed through the business, gaining a reputation for delivery, ultimately resulting in my promotion to Partner in 2004.

My passion for helping others led me towards furthering my career in learning & development and I set up my own consultancy in 2009, through which I'm committed to helping individuals perform at their best at work. I've worked with hundreds of people on large programmes and in individual sessions, all designed to help them raise their performance.

It's really important to me that everything I do is practical and reflects the world of the professional – usually extremely busy fee earners who are focused on delivering to clients.

So, here's the book I wish I'd had in my back pocket.

Your practical, hands on guide to help you move from technical expert to manager.

I wish you luck on your journey.

Sue Willcock, Director, Chaseville Consulting Ltd.

Introduction

You've spent years training to be an expert in your field.

You've probably completed a degree, followed by some post-graduate qualifications and quite likely a final exam which marked the final leg on your journey to become a 'Professional'. An Accountant, an Engineer, a Surveyor, a Solicitor, an IT Professional…

You've written essays late into the night on the science and art of your chosen profession and by now have quite a bit of experience. You keep up to date by reading, attending lectures and working with people you admire.

You've now become pretty good at the job that you once aspired to do.

So good, in fact, that you have been asked to stop doing it all the time.

You've been asked to manage a team.

You now have to assess people, develop them, judge their performance and help them deliver results for your organisation.

But all that studying, time spent learning and delivering for clients was not really about people management. It was about applying your technical knowledge.

Of course, you have dealt with people and someone obviously thinks you are quite good at it – hence they trust you with managing and leading others.

But now you have a new role.

Now, you have to appraise, give feedback and help others perform at their best. You have to inspire them.

You already know there are quite a few skills that you have picked up during your career that will be useful. You can certainly run a meeting and you have often defined objectives whilst working with clients, so there's definitely some stuff that you can do standing on your head.

But, if you are anything like the many professionals I work with, you don't just want to 'do the job' – you want to rise to the challenge and do it well.

And you need to move fast.

You are being watched by your manager and your team and they are waiting for your next move.

For your team members, it may be quite a shift – it may be that you were once their peer and now you are their manager. Will you change? What will your 'management style' be to get results?

And of course, alongside this, you've still got to clients to keep happy. How on earth will you make the time to get all this done?

This is the book you need to get you started on your journey.

There's no MBA required – it's a simple and practical guide that will help you manage your team and your time whilst continuing to deliver to clients.

Through this book I'll share with you the things I have done, with success, in in my own career as a manager and leader within the professional services sector. I'll share the tips I learnt from working alongside Managing Partners, CEOs and Directors, and success stories gathered from working with technical professionals who, like you, had just taken on a manager role.

I'll also tell you some stories of the things I have done that did not go so well, so that you can avoid some of the pitfalls.

I know that taking on a new manager role can be lonely – you need to find your feet and learn new skills very quickly, whilst being under more scrutiny than ever before.

Often, it will take some bravery to get better.

The book is deliberately to the point, practical and full of 'knowledge nuggets' that you can take, adapt and make your own.

I hope you find it to be the 'friend in your back pocket' during your initial steps into management.

I'M A MANAGER

*A practical **guide to success** as a **first time** people manager in **professional** services.*

Chapter 1

Identify your web for success

So, you have left the office on Friday knowing that on Monday you are returning as a manager. What does this mean? Do you need to buy a new suit? Do you need to stop telling jokes in meetings? It may well mean these things over time, but let's assume for now that you look the part and have been appointed because someone believes in you.

Your first six weeks in the job are critical. Whatever the state of your team (brand new or established) as a new manager, you now operate in a different world. You have new responsibilities and the focus of your job has shifted or, at the very least, broadened.

This first chapter will help you explore and build a robust new world by helping you identify the web, or network, you need in place to be successful.

Know that the fundamentals of good performance both for you and your team, will very much depend on the creation of productive relationships.

If you do nothing else in your first few weeks than start to create a strong web of productive relationships – i.e. those that will help you be successful, then you will be off to a good start.

If you are wondering what I mean by a 'productive relationship', rest assured that you already know what one looks and feels like. Just think about your best boss, best flatmate, best friend – and then think about what it is that makes the relationship productive (not just 'nice', but 'productive').

I expect your list is likely to include mutual trust, valuing each other's opinion, honesty and openness. These are the things you need to create with a group of people that will help you to be successful in your new role.

The challenge here is to consciously create the network you now need. Who do you need around you to be successful? I invite you to begin to draw your new web now. **It will be different to the one you had yesterday when you were not a manager - and that's the point.**

You may decide to create two webs – one showing your current web and another that is aspirational.

Webs should include you in the middle and then, at relative distance to you, your line manager, your team and your peers. You may find it useful to include your partner at home, family, friends, clients and current or potential buddies or mentors.

As you create your web of success, ask yourself these questions:

- Who do I need around me to be successful?

- What kind of relationship do I need with each person? It's useful to write this on the line linking you to them (e.g. 'sounding board for new ideas', 'HR support', 'give me confidence to try new things'.)

- Where is this relationship now? (E.g. is it new or established, does it need to be developed?).

- What do I need to do to make this a 'productive relationship' in the context of my new role?

- What is the difference between what I have now and what I need to be successful?

- Do I need to identify a specific mentor, buddy or coach?

Every time I undertake this exercise with clients, particularly with those in transitionary roles, I see light bulb moments happen.

This is not about being mercenary – "I need to be best friends with the CEO to be successful" is not what I am getting at here.

The point is that your role has shifted and the web that served you well as a technical expert is not likely to serve you as well now that you are a manager.

I have included a sample web on the next page to help you draw your own.

The process you go through and the thinking you put into this is much more important than it looking lovely, as you can see from the one here.

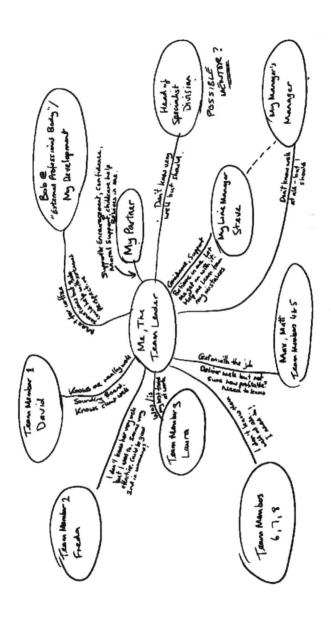

Once you have given thought to your 'web for success' your next step needs to be to start creating it in reality – building strong relationships with your team members, your line manager and others that you identified as being critical to your success.

This does not just mean taking everyone out for a beer.

Neither does it mean you telling them what you need from them. You should be looking to genuinely create strong relationships that are productive for both of you.

The next two chapters give you some more guidance on how to get the new web working.

Coffee break highlights

o The network that served you as a technical professional is unlikely to serve you well on your journey into management.

o Consider your new network, with you at the centre. Who you need around you to be successful?

o The process of creating the web is as important as the final result as it encourages you ask yourself some critical questions about your new world.

Chapter 2

Relationships in the first six weeks

Part of your web of success is almost certainly going to include team members, your own line manager and people in your life who will support you.

For this reason, I've dedicated a whole chapter to the four things to do in your first six weeks as a manager, in relation to these people.

Some of you may already be thinking *'I don't have time'* so if this is you, then I'd urge you to think about the purpose of your new role.

In a nutshell, as a manager, your job is to deliver business results not just by yourself, but through others too. Your job is to apply your skill and expertise to help others perform at their best.

I am hesitating to get out my 'Corporate Business Bingo' card and say that you must 'elicit extra effort from your team' or 'create a high performing team that delivers added value', as I want this to be a jargon free book – but these phrases are in fact very valid.

Perhaps one of the best ways of getting this point across is through my first 'been there done it' tip.

Leverage, I will admit, is a word I only started to understand later in my career. In truth, I was a bit late to the 'leverage' party.

One definition of 'leverage' is to influence something (a system, or an environment, or dare I say, a group of people), in a way that multiplies the outcome of your effort without a corresponding increase in the resources used.

The reason I like to use the word in relation to the management role is that junior managers, in particular, don't consider leverage as part of their role.

But it's critical.

Put simply, if I manage 10 people, it is better for the business for me to help these 10 do their job very well than to just focus my time on my clients or projects - because I cannot do the job of 10 people.

My results as an individual are amplified if I focus my effort on the team doing a great job.

You can leverage your own capability by managing your team well.

This is simplistic and for some will be stating the

obvious.

I mention it however, because I see countless new managers trying to fit in their management role as an 'added extra' and I think they (and sometimes their organisations) are missing the point.

So, as you approach this chapter and your role at large, a question to consider is:

"How can I best spend my time today to leverage my skills through my team?"

This may lead to many answers – one of which I hope will be to spend time nurturing relationships in your team to help people perform at their best.

With the issue of leverage in mind, here are **4 things to do in the first six weeks** with your developing network.

Once you have read these through, I strongly recommend you make a plan with your diary alongside you as to how you will make these happen.

1) **Seek to get to know your team members for yourself.**

   Don't take anyone's word for the worthiness or effectiveness of a team member. Watch, observe and meet with them individually and as a group. Make sure these interactions include conversations that really matter. These are outlined in Chapter 3.

2) **Take time out to think about the team you have.**

   How do they work together? What skills do they have? What motivates each person? Keep a record of your thoughts that you can refer back to as the depth of your understanding grows. It's highly likely that your opinion will shift as you discover more about your team and being able to test new ideas against earlier observations can be invaluable in assessing how you need to help your team to grow.

3) **Make the time to speak with your own line manager.**

   It's key that you're crystal clear on your responsibilities and your line manager's expectations of you and your team.

Schedule a meeting with him/her as soon as you can with the intent of agreeing what is expected of you. Chapter 4 covers this in more detail, but for now, know that there may well be things that they expect you to do now that you just did not realise. Make sure you know what they are early on. These may be as mundane as approving holidays or signing off timesheets, but all will have an impact on your time and the perceived effectiveness of you in role. Personally, I think it's lame to say "oh, I didn't know I needed to do that" after 6 weeks. You have a responsibility to ask and find out.

Once you are clear on what's expected of you, find out about the resources you have to help you. You may not need to know the detail of the appraisal process yet, but you may need to know when you are supposed to review people, when pay rises happen, where the information might be to help you manage a performance issue. Are you responsible for providing information upwards that is new to you?

The conversation must cover not just what they expect you to do, but how they expect you to do it. Do they want you to report back every week on your progress, or just ask for help when needed? Are they expecting to be copied in on all your team e-mails? Which bits of their role do they want you to make work better for them?

 *To be noticed, a great strategy is to become a go-to person for your own line manager. You need to be the first person they think of when something needs doing. Convert this into a powerful question and, early on, ask your own manager,*

"What's the most useful thing I can do to make your life easier?"

4) Identify a colleague who can support you

Find someone who has "been there, done it" and ask them to help you. This does not have to be a formal buddy but just someone who is willing to answer questions from "where do I sign this holiday form?" to "I had a rubbish day with my team, can I talk it over with you?"

Remember, in the first six weeks, you must stay focused on creating a bedrock upon which you can start to become the manager you want to be. Your aim is to discover the skill, motivations, strengths and weaknesses of the team you have in comparison to the team you need. That is, the team you need to deliver on the promises you are simultaneously understanding and making to your line manager.

In the coming months, you will need to set objectives, motivate, inspire and move your team forward.

Aim to do this based on the bedrock of trust and relationships that you start to build in the first four to six weeks.

Experience would tell me to promise nothing in the first six weeks unless you are *absolutely sure* you can deliver. You want to start to build a reputation as someone who delivers on their promises - so be careful what you promise. Statements like "I can get you a pay rise" if in fact there is a six step process to go through will come back with big teeth to bite you if they don't happen.

As you develop your own management style, and depending on your organisation's culture, you may well find that you do need to curb the jokes, buy a posh suit or a new flashy pen to elevate your personal impact and presence. Though we may not like it, people do respond to what we look like and our decorum and gravitas around others.

But, I would suggest that's not for now. Turning up with a new look on day one or trying to be someone you are not is, in my view, too much like hard work when you have real work to do and detracts from the objective to build trust, especially if people knew you before.

I once worked with a guy who, newly promoted, came in with black hair, freshly dyed from his wispy grey locks on the Friday.

Don't do it people.

Coffee break highlights

o Get to know your team members as individuals – their aspirations, motivations and expectations of you. Don't make assumptions.

o Know what your line manager expects from you in terms of what you do and how you do it.

o Seek out a buddy to help you.

o Ask yourself 'How can I best spend my time today to leverage my skills through my team?'

o Remember, you are aiming to build a bedrock of trust.

Chapter 3

Have conversations that matter

Having studied for years for an MBA, it's slightly ironic that one of the most enlightening career conversations for me took place in a pub in Kings Cross, London, when a soon-to-be boss sat me down over a drink.

I was already in a management position so was expecting a conversation around my future to-do-list and induction process but as it turned out, this was a conversation about the 'how' – how we both liked to work – not the what.   Until that point, we'd met once at interview so knew each other pretty superficially at "I interviewed well and looked smart in a suit" level.

In that brief interaction, using an approach similar to the one I outline in this chapter, my new manager had what he needed to help me perform at my best. And I had what I needed to know in terms of working with him. In the space of an hour, we were well on the way to developing a trusting working relationship.

Not bad for the price of a beer.

Maybe you have inherited a team from someone else, or you are recruiting. Either way, this level of conversation, to be had individually with your team members as soon as possible after you become their manager, can avoid many dramas or challenges you may otherwise have when working together.

You should also endeavour to have this type conversation with your own line manager.

Of course, you don't have to have this conversation just with a new starter – you can do what my American friends call a "do over" – just start from scratch with someone if you think you need to. It can of course involve a beer, if that works for you (or afternoon tea - or whatever takes your fancy to create an environment for informality). The only point I would make here is to pick somewhere that's not too noisy so you can have a decent conversation without shouting at each other!

What is a 'conversation that matters'?

Essentially, this type of conversation involves getting to know your team member at a level beyond the superficial. This is about you and them. Not about projects, clients or tasks.

You may have this type of conversation with your team members already, but it may have taken you a few months or years to get to this point – it needn't.

The outcome you are looking for from this conversation is **how** you will work together so you are both at your best and to start to build trust.

I am resisting the temptation to give you a script – as a professional reading this book, I doubt you need one.

Instead, here are some pointers as to the areas you might cover.

Being yourself is a critical element of building trust so please take the time to make these your own style – maybe practice with friends or your buddy and pace the conversation to suit you and the person you are talking to.

Share with them...

What you value in life e.g. family, friends, career, honesty, integrity, fairness…

How your values show themselves. Tell them the positives and the negatives. For example, "*I leave early on Tuesdays to take my son to football*" or "*Sometimes I get very engrossed in my work and you* *might think I am ignoring you, I am not, I just like getting things right and need to focus."*

Things that drive you nuts. This builds on how your values show themselves, e.g. *"I get really angry if I see someone not showing respect to others as it's really important to me.", "I can't stand lateness as I think it is disrespectful".*

How you think you work at your best and how you would like to work together. Don't use clichés here e.g. *"don't come to me with a problem, come with a solution"* is a bit of a hackneyed phrase! Be honest, open and aim to help them to help you work at your best. My own examples as a manager, would include:

- *Tell me if you have made a mistake so I am forearmed if someone mentions it to me directly.*

- *If I don't check in with you often enough, just tell me.*

- *Don't be afraid to give me feedback. I'd rather hear it, than not.*

- *Be really clear on what you want from any 1:1s we have and come with a list of outcomes that you want or decisions you need.*

This is a two-way conversation though. Ask them the same things and, most critically listen well to their responses. This means truly listening so that you can interpret what they say into how you will build a strong working relationship.

Your own level of sharing and disclosure will model the way for them and it needs to be at a level that is comfortable for both of you.

To recap, you are asking them:

- **What they value**

- **How their values show themselves**

- **Things that drive them nuts and why**

- **How they work at their best and how they would like to work together.**

Alongside your own responses, you can start to explore how you will create a productive working relationship and discuss potential clashes.

This should be a natural conversation so may not happen in one sitting. It is supremely valuable though.

Some outcomes I have seen from this type of conversation include a team member telling their manager things like:

- *I value thinking time and like to get out of the office to walk if I have a problem to solve.*

- *I value bouncing ideas off of other people so often find it useful to chat to people over a coffee.*

- *I am really confident in my peer group but get nervous around people of authority so may need support in this area.*

- *I would like to pick my son up from school at least once a week.*

- *Please give me clear objectives and then let me get on with them. I'll shout if I have a problem.*

- *Please don't give me a blank sheet of paper to do what I like with. I like direction and an end goal that I can work to.*

- *I can do detail if I need to, but prefer someone else to check and read over things as I find it dull – this means I am not actually very good at it.*

What you are effectively doing here is starting to

explore the 'behavioural iceberg' (worth a Google if you want to know more) looking at underlying values and things that are important to each of you.

Trust me, this will short cut you to greater effectiveness.

Be yourself and be natural. You may take a few attempts to feel comfortable asking some of these questions or giving away your own information. That's OK. This is not a counselling session; it's about building a productive working relationship. If you need help starting, you might say something like:

"For us to work together really well, I thought it would be useful to know a bit more about what makes you tick and for me to share how I work at my best too."

Depending on your personality and the other person's openness, experience and level of self-awareness, it may take you more than one conversation to get to all of these issues – trust your instincts and pace it.

The outcome you are looking for is to build a relationship based on trust and so keep this authentic to you. You may not want to share your deepest thoughts and secrets and that's perfectly acceptable. Even if you start by focusing on how you like to work, not the what, that is a valuable start.

The benefits of this approach are:

- If you spot a behaviour that you personally think is odd, or at odds with your organization, you have some idea as to where it is coming from and can have a more productive conversation about how to deal with it.

- You can start to understand what motivates your team member so you can set challenging objectives and help develop their career.

- It deepens trust on which to develop and build a good working relationship.

Here, I have focused on having conversations that matter with your team member, but as outlined in the previous chapter, you should look to get yourself into a position to have this type of conversation with your own line manager too. Knowing what matters to them alongside their expectations of you is critical to your success.

Coffee break highlights

o 'Conversations that matter' focus on how people like to work – not the what and when of projects and clients.

o You should be looking to have natural two-way conversations about what is important to each of you and how this might play itself out at work.

o The aim is to start to build a productive working relationship.

o Don't rush in with your size 11 boots – be yourself, let the other person be themselves and pace these types of conversation to make them count.

o To make a start, you might say something like, "For us to work together really well, I thought it would be useful to know a bit more about what makes you tick and for me to share how I work at my best too."

Chapter 4

What's expected?

As I've mentioned previously, when you take on the role of manager (indeed, ideally before you are in role), you should know and understand very clearly what is expected of you.

Although I feel like this statement is blindingly obvious, I am a realist – I know there have been times in my own career when I have not really known what is expected of me and indeed, when I have not been clear to others.

I've turned up at work, done lots of 'stuff', been 'busy' and rushed around a lot with a notebook and laptop. Back to back meetings.

Busy. Busy. Busy.

But, like many of us at different times in our lives, I can be a busy fool.

I can always find things to do, for clients, for the business or for my team.

So, let's get one thing out of the way really early. There are no excuses on this one. You must know what is expected of you.

This is why I have dedicated a whole chapter to this area.

You now have the word 'Manager' (or maybe even 'Leader') in your job description. Just as you have responsibilities to clients, you now have a responsibility to your team.

A massive part of this is agreeing with them what they will achieve and how they will achieve it. To do this, you need to know what is expected of you too - both in terms of tasks and behaviour. Some of the businesses you work in may measure you on these and use words like 'technical and behavioural competencies'.

These can be complicated beasts of documents so let's just say you will be measured both on 'what you do and the way you do it'.

Your business may well have frameworks in place to help you know what these are and if so, get hold of the relevant framework right now.

As well as this being about what is expected of you early on, when it comes to the management of your team, you will need to review existing performance objectives or set some new ones, and we look at this in more detail in the next chapter.

For now, though, I invite you to think about what the expectations are of you in your new role.

These will be specific to your organisation but as a guide and for use in your conversation with your line manager (and then with your teams) here's a simple checklist to get you thinking about the expectations of you as a manager in professional services. I've kept these short and broad – you are urged to find out what the specific expectations are in your role and convert these into SMART objectives (more of these later) with your own line manager.

What you do

- Deliver a quality service to clients directly and through your team.

- Sell – by winning new work, through repeat business or by developing new services/products.

- Deliver results on broader business projects.

- Motivate people to perform and deal with poor performers.

- Recruit and induct new people.

- Set team objectives.

- Maintain quality standards and legal compliance.

- Develop yourself and your team members.

- Manage a budget.

- Write and stick to a business plan.

The way you do it

As well as your manager duties above, this area is probably where the expectations of you have shifted the most - the 'web of success' that you created earlier will help you with this too.

You must find out what kinds of behaviours are important in your own organisation. To get you thinking, some of the most useful 'behaviours of a manager' I've observed over the years are:

- Being a role model for expected behaviour in the business (e.g. on time for meetings, always say thanks, look the part as appropriate to your business, be positive about the future, celebrate success).

- Being a brand ambassador. No rubbishing the company, being positive even in the face of change, being a positive influence on others and 'selling' the brand to newcomers.

- Inspiring your team to perform through your own behaviour. Don't be a 'mood hoover'.

- Challenging the way things are done in the spirit of genuine improvement.

- Asking for and freely giving feedback – again in the spirit of genuine improvement.

- Creating relationships with others that engender trust.

- Leading the way with innovation and new ideas that take the business forward.

Please don't wait to be told what is expected of you.

If you are lucky, there will be a job description for you to follow but even if this exists, you still need specific objectives and expectations to be agreed with your own line manager so you can 'get your ducks all in a row' to deliver – managing your time and your team to deliver results.

If you have no job description, or (worse still) a disinterested line manager yourself, aim to be the 'breaker in the waves' – so you don't carry their disinterest and disengagement down to your team.

Write your own objectives, play them back to your line manager and then cascade them down.

Travelling in a direction that is roughly right is much better than being directionless for six months as it gives you a platform for decisions and your team some chance of autonomy.

Coffee break highlights

- There are no excuses – you must find out what is expected of you and your team. And fast. Preferably know this before you take on your new role.

- Agree with your line manager both what you need to do and the way they (and the broader business) would like it to be done. The latter may be implied, or may need to be discussed. Getting stuff done in professional services whilst getting the nickname 'Wolf of Wall Street' is probably not the best way to go.

- If you have a line manager that could be better, consider how you could be the 'breaker in the waves' for your team.

Chapter 5

Know that you are learning

So far, we've covered what your new role is, what is expected of you and a little of what your new world might look and feel like.

At this point, I invite you to take a breath and reflect on the journey you are on.

As those of us who have studied to learn a profession know only too well, the key to doing something well is often to find out how others have done it (either by reading, watching, talking or listening), giving it a go for ourselves and then learning from our experience.

It always amazes me that many people think that management is somehow different. They expect to become a good manager without applying the same approach to learning. Perhaps it is because as new managers we feel more exposed and 'on show' than ever before.

I know some people think that because they have the title, they have the competence (when sometimes they don't). I know others that just feel like a cheat and undeserved of the title. And I know many people in between.

Wherever you may be on this scale as a new manager, please know that you are learning a new skill and it requires the same effort, resilience and reflection as it took for you to become the technical professional that you already are.

And that's OK.

But, as a new manager, you now have a responsibility to lead and manage others in your business. This means you have a responsibility to invest in your own development to be the best manager you can be. You will also need to develop others in your team, often without access to a formal budget.

This chapter is designed to help you identify how you will further your own development even if you have scant time or financial resources. Of course, you can pass these ideas on to your team members too (useful for when you are having developmental conversations), but primarily these are written for you as a new manager.

In my experience, many consultancies are still cautious of spending vast sums on training budgets. As a new manager, you may be lucky enough to be a delegate on an in-house development programme or you may have a mentor or a coach.

Even if you don't have this luxury, this does not mean you do not have a responsibility to your team to develop yourself as a manager and to help them as part of their own progression.

Accept the fact that you are learning a new role and give yourself permission to learn.

Just like when you learnt many of the technical aspects of your job and made mistakes, you will once again make mistakes.

Simply knowing this helped me to take more risks as a new manager and whilst I would never say I was reckless (not many people I know who train to be a Quantity Surveyor, as I did originally, would qualify as reckless!), it gave me the confidence to say, "I am going to try this today and see what happens."

Reflect on your mistakes and ask yourself what you will do to achieve something different next time.

Here are some ways you can develop yourself right now, as part of your journey into management and leadership.

They are all free or very low cost but will require

you to spend time on them, and, at times to 'be brave'.

- **Actively seek feedback on your performance.** A great way of identifying areas to develop yourself and identifying strengths to build on is simply to ask for feedback. Whilst a formal 360 feedback process can be very valuable, you can just ask those around you to give you feedback.

- **Get out of your comfort zone.** If getting completely out of your comfort zone is too uncomfortable, set yourself a target which builds on an area where you already have strengths, and then use this to structure your planned development. Make sure you set a clearly defined goal so you know when you've reached it too. For example, if you are OK at writing project reports but want to be brilliant, how will you know what 'brilliant' is? (Feedback, benchmarks with others etc.). Once you know 'what good looks like', you can then plan how to get there.

- **Consider the Performance-Image-Exposure (PIE) model and how it applies to you**. The PIE model developed by Harvey Coleman and presented in his book 'Empowering Yourself – The Organisational Game Revealed', suggests that our success at work depends on our performance (10%), image (30%) and exposure (60%). For those of us who trained technically, this is often a depressing model to ponder, but I know when I have talked about it as a speaker at Chartered Institute of Building (CIOB) CPD events, I end up with a few nods in the room as people recall the individuals at work who get promoted. One of the reasons I spend time talking about your network for success in this book is because of the PIE model.

- With this model in mind, **you could now review your network for success,** looking at where you want to take your career and who you can learn from to help you get there. Are there people with specialist knowledge that you could learn from? Are there 'types' of people missing (e.g. do you need to surround yourself with more entrepreneurs/risk takers/creatives?)

- **Find some learning buddies**. As I mention in Chapter 1, creating your web for success does not mean befriending people in a shallow way just to meet you own ends. What knowledge might you share with someone in return for them teaching you a new skill or giving you their expert opinion? How might you create a buddy relationship to support development for you both?

- **Use social media**. Many sectors use social media much more than others to learn from colleagues outside their immediate networks (the IT sector is one that springs to mind). Online forums can be an invaluable source of learning. Special interest forums on Linked-In, together with specific websites for your sector (websites associated with sector magazines usually have good discussion forums) will help keep you up to date. Follow your professional institution on Facebook, Linked In and Twitter alongside leadership and management bodies such as Harvard Business Review (they post great articles) and the Chartered Management Institute – to name just two.

- **Explore iTunes, YouTube and TED Talks for learning**. If you haven't discovered these online learning tools, then go exploring right now.

- **Discover audio books.** Audio books on Audible.com or other such sites are well worth investigating. Especially if you are a professional on the move - audio books can be a great way of learning. I find a combination of audio books, a speaker pillow (yes, it really is a pillow with an in-built speaker) and downloads on my smartphone for the car mean I can often 'read' a book a week.

- **Use libraries and other public resources.** OK, so Amazon makes it easy to order books for delivery direct to your door, but a visit to the library not only provides a quiet space for thinking, but by simply browsing around can spark thoughts and new lines of thinking. The British Library at Euston, London is one of my favourite places and has a fantastic business centre with regular seminars taking place. Likewise, local libraries are also great resources for self-development (and quiet space). Museums also very often have free entry or specific events that are reasonably priced and may be aligned to your learning goals.

- **Question your newspaper, radio and TV choices.** Challenge your thinking by questioning your reading, viewing and listening habits by changing for a while and tuning in to new things. Turning up to a work having just about managed to flick through 'Metro' might be better replaced by reading an industry magazine, listened to in-depth news on Radio 4 or having browsed a quality newspaper online.

- **Go to the free exhibitions attached to conferences.** Many of us receive invites to exhibition/conferences where the ticket price is often prohibitive to attending. My advice here is to weigh up the networking opportunities and the exhibition (think about the PIE model), know who the exhibitors are and plan your day in advance to meet and mingle to meet your needs by just attending the free bit. Often you pick up lots of free learning material from exhibitors and gain immense value from the free seminars and networking. Just be clear on your objectives before attending.

- **Plants & nature**. There is some evidence to suggest that that plants on our desks are beneficial when working – reducing stress and increasing creativity for some. Beyond the office environment, being close to nature can also help you process information, slow down and reflect.   You may not feel that you will work better because there is a plant on your desk, but I think we have all had the feeling that we need fresh air, or to get out of the office and see some greenery to help us think. Reflecting is a really important part of the learning process so don't underestimate what getting close to nature can do for you.

As the saying goes, "If you always do what you've always done, you will always get what you've always got". So, to achieve different results, you must explore doing things differently. Some of my best personal development happens when:

- *I jump (or am pushed) out of my comfort zone.*

- *I step up and take responsibility for my own development.   I have dedicated significant weekends and sums of money to learning.   I read lots of books. I subscribe to management and sector specific magazines.*

- *I adopt a 'be brave' mind-set.   This means*

being brave enough to try and new approach in a team meeting, being brave enough to ask for feedback or (for me) being brave enough to connect with someone who, without my 'brave head' on, I may not even speak to.

Coffee break highlights

○ Accept that you are learning. This means it's OK to try something, reflect on it, get feedback and try it again to get better – just like you did when you were training as a professional.

○ If you are short of a budget, this does not give you an excuse to short-change your team and not be the best manager you can be. After all, you accepted the role.

○ Know the Performance-Image-Exposure model and think about how to apply it for success as a manager.

○ Ask for feedback.

○ Find a buddy.

○ Use resources that work for you to broaden your thinking. Books, conferences, exhibitions, libraries, newspapers, audio books, YouTube etc.

Chapter 6

Meaningful goals for the team

I have to say that the thought of setting objectives and then appraising people against them used to fill me with dread.

My first stab at it saw me take the approach of undertaking a very comprehensive 'school report'. I diligently took the company's standard appraisal form, issued blanks ahead of time with a note asking people to think about their objectives, and make notes before we met.

People turned up, we talked for about an hour, I told them about the business plan I had written (which they had all contributed to) and I then divided up the tasks in the business plan into their roles.

There was no way we were not achieving the plan and if there was one item not done, I would be able to pinpoint who had not delivered.

I remember writing the appraisals up over one weekend by hand and leaving them all in personalised envelopes on desks ready for a signature, filing and a review every month.

You'd have to ask my team members of the day how they felt about this approach when I did it, but my own observations, with the benefit of more experience and hindsight are:

What was good

- Boy, were those objectives clear. If we did not meet them, I sure knew who was accountable.

- The objectives were all really well aligned to a team plan. All for one and one for all and all that.

- They all had the business plan. I think I even copied it and attached it to their personal objectives. Just to be really clear. They all knew which bit each other were responsible for. That was good for the team.

- I did them all. On time.

What was not so good

- I stuck to the form. Really rigidly. Probably from fear! I don't recall asking what they wanted or having a deliberate conversation about how we could best use their talents or what motivated them.

- I wrote their goals for them. This was bad for

three reasons:

- o Firstly, because I lost a weekend to writing up my lovely 'school reports'.

- o Secondly, studies I have read since have told me that ownership of goals is better if someone writes them themselves. In their own words. If I had got my team to do this, it's likely I would have increased their ownership.

- o Finally, getting people to write down goals and play them back to you means you can ensure you are agreeing to the thing you think you have agreed.

- It was all a bit 'parent-child' – whilst the approach brought about the benefits above, I look back and think I was being a bit parent-y! Maybe the more experienced members of my team wanted to tell me where to shove my school reports. They just never told me.

To be fair, we had a good year as a team. So something worked. But the lessons from this, and those I have learnt since, are:

- You don't need a form to set someone goals.

- Goals should be jointly owned. They are their goals, not yours. Your job is to make sure they are goals that are aligned to what your team needs to do and what your organisation needs from the individual.

- Whilst we all have to do some stuff at work we really don't like, most of us turn up to do a good job and do things that in the most part mean we enjoy our time at work. If you are having conversations that matter, you will know what motivates your team members. Play to this.

- Sometimes, it is your job to be the person that pushes someone outside their comfort zone. But do this with support and realism. If you are pushing someone and they are getting so stressed that they are lying awake at night, then you need to deal with that. If you are pushing someone, giving them support and they are coming in to work puffed up with pride at their new found skill and growing in confidence, then great.

The thought of setting goals for others may well fill you with dread. I find it's often the biggest thing new managers find difficult – perhaps because it is one of the things where you feel you are a 'manager' for the first time and have a 'proper responsibility' to others.

Or perhaps because when others have set objectives for you, they may have been done badly, so you have no role models of what it could really be like?

Whatever the reason, this chapter is aimed at helping you feel positive about setting goals and to help you plan for success when sitting down with an individual in your team.

If you are nervous, think of the goal setting meeting as simply having another 'conversation that matters'. It is really just about having a conversation about what they want and what you and the company needs from them.

Remember, the best conversations happen when you have a productive relationship with the other person. You should be cultivating this relationship all the time.

I was once in a tricky situation of managing a relative of one of the Directors in an organisation.

Unfortunately, this person was not performing. After taking a bravery pill, I had a conversation which simply started with, 'I have an appraisal form in front of me but instead of going through that, why don't we just have a chat about you? I have seen you getting to work late, looking despondent and unhappy and the report you did last week was not what I think you are capable of. Shall we talk about what's going on?'

The talk was productive and one of the most memorable of my career as he admitted he was doing what he was expected to do by his family, not what he wanted to do. With some more support and follow up, he left to follow his chosen career and return to college. Yes, he left. It was the best outcome for him, the team and the business.

Always remember, you are simply talking to another human being. They have a life outside work which, for most people, gives them a reason to come in every day and do their job in a certain way.

Ignore the whole person at your peril.

An easy way to think about setting meaningful objectives is to consider three parts to the conversation.

When you are 'live' undertaking an appraisal, if you have a blank moment, just remember you want to get to the end of year and say "We D-I-D it!" This will help remind you of the three elements of a good goal setting session - Delivery, Inspiration and Development – which we will explore now.

Delivery

Firstly, think about what the business needs from you and them in the coming 6-12 months. What outcomes do you need to deliver? This is a good place to start because it stops you having some kind of fluffy conversation about 'how things are going'.

If you do not have a full picture, what do you know that is certain? Do you know they are on a project that lasts until a certain time, do you know the client has another project they would love them to work on? What might they work on that will tie to Inspiring and Developing them as a person and for the business?

INSPIRATION

What do they want from the business? Do they want to be a technically brilliant expert, get closer to clients, gain experience in a certain sector? What do they want to get from their time with your organisation? Most people come to work to make a difference in some way. A good question to ask is what difference they want to feel they have made, when they go home at the end of each day. Money is just not enough to make people work hard or smart, so what else do you give them? What gets them out of bed in the morning and choose to work for you over your competitors? Can you give them more of that?

DEVELOPMENT

The third level is very much all about the individual. What do they need to do to grow technically and professionally in your organisation? This is not all about spending money on courses.

Yes, external help is often invaluable, but mentoring, buddying and working alongside a more experienced individual, doing a project that covers new ground or adding appropriate responsibility to their role can all be covered by their objectives.

The specifics within the Delivery-Inspiration-Development model will depend on the individual and the business need, but ideas that may spark some thought include:

- Giving someone a challenging project to work on.

- Moving them to a new sector/client/ service line to apply current knowledge in a new way.

- Asking a more experienced member of staff to develop a trainee.

- Secondments to other departments.

- Creating a plan to become the business expert on a specialist topic.

- Taking on some management responsibility.

- Leading team meetings.

- Becoming an external speaker on a topic that will benefit the marketing and sales efforts of the firm.

Finally, a word about **SMART** objectives.

SMART is a well-known acronym used to help set great goals and objectives. It stands for objectives that are:

Specific (Do X, specifically)

Measureable (enough to know when you have reached the goal)

Agreed (between you and the other person)

Realistic (i.e. achievable)

Time-related (e.g. to a deadline or timescale)

It's a memorable model which is best used alongside the **D-I-D** framework, as a way to hone down the final objectives you agree.

It can take some thought to create a SMART objective but, without one, you can easily get yourself into a 'bite on the rear' situation when it comes to fairly assessing someone's success.

By way of example, think of a discussion with Fred the Team Member based on the following objectives.

How well do you think each meeting would progress if you were New Manager 1 and New Manager 2?

"So, Fred, we are going to review your performance for the last few months. Let's talk about whether you met the goals we agreed."

New Manager 1 has to base his conversation on these goals.

1. Deliver Project Zebedee.

2. Write the new guidelines for dealing with client complaints.

3. Make sure all invoices go out on time and are paid.

New Manager 2 has to base his conversation on these goals.

1. Deliver Project Zebedee in order that we deliver a 7% profit by the end of the project in 10 months' time. Your target is also to win at least one piece of repeat business with this client over the course of this project and to

maintain or exceed our 8/10 customer satisfaction score with this client.

2. Create our new guidelines for dealing with client complaints. This should be completed in draft in 2 months' time, allowing time for a review and sign off by the Board. The Guidelines are to be live on our website on March 1st.

3. Prepare and arrange internal sign off of invoices so that they are all issued to clients by the 5th day of each month. Monitor payment of the invoices and provide a report of debtors (detailing reasons for any unpaid invoices) on the 30th of each month for the Board Meeting on the 1st of each month.

Although the latter, SMART objectives can take longer to create and agree, think about how much easier it is to Deliver, Inspire and Develop your team using a SMART objective.

It's also easier to monitor these over time so that evaluation is made simpler.

The level to which you co-write objectives will depend on the experience, capability and motivation of your team members – for some members of your team, you may just need to give guidance and ask them to create the objectives with your sign off.

For others, more intervention and support may be required. In all cases, however, they must be agreed between the two of you and don't forget to update them if things change.

Coffee break highlights

○ The process of setting goals is a really powerful tool in the manager's toolkit.

○ Goal setting conversations are made easier if you have built a productive relationship with your team member.

○ If your mind goes blank in a goal setting conversation, just remember, you want to be able to look back and say "we DID it". Set goals that are about:

Delivery, **I**nspiring the other person and their **D**evelopment.

○ Take the time to work with the other person to make their goals SMART. Trust me, it will make both your lives easier.

○ The level to which you have to help someone create agreed goals will depend on their capability and their motivation.

Chapter 7

Manage with outcomes

Many years ago, when I was a developing manager, I was told by an experienced leader that I was viewing an issue I was grappling with through the 'wrong end of the telescope'. I had entered the conversation hoping for some specific advice, but instead had got an analogy about telescopes. It was not quite what I was looking for.

Later, however, I reflected on his comment as being one of the most useful pieces of advice I've ever been given in my career.

The 'outcome approach' invites you to always look at the horizon at the end of the telescope, before commencing with the detail of what you do. In other words, clearly identify the outcome you are trying to achieve, before you look at the tasks that make it up.

Whilst this can easily sit alongside objective setting, I have dedicated a whole chapter to outcomes as I believe this way of thinking is so powerful. Indeed, it can be life-changing.

My favourite definition of this approach comes from a group of delegates I worked with a few years ago.

Taking an outcome approach means…

What you do and the way that you do it should be influenced by the outcome you are trying to achieve.

This transcends everything you do a manager – for clients, for your team, for yourself. Even at home. When undertaking any task, you need to first understand the ultimate result that you are trying to achieve.

Turn your telescope around and see what the outcome is on the horizon.

Most people I know will have given some thought to what they might want to achieve in the coming year - either personally, professionally or both. For many of us though, we might have made plans in the past only for them to gather dust, metaphorically or literally on our desks, perhaps leaving us with a sense of under-achievement or (at the least) a bit demotivated.

This approach helps you to make your plans meaningful for you, your business and your team members by focusing first on the outcome you are trying to achieve - i.e. the 'why', before moving onto the 'what' and 'how'.

For those of your who have read Stephen Covey's work, the phrase '*beginning with the end in mind*' may well spring to mind from his book, 'The 7 Habits of Highly Effective People'.

Reasons that this 'outcome approach' works are:

- It focuses on why you are doing something and in the process filters out 'noise' and 'stuff' that might otherwise distract you.

- It helps make your goals positive - you will be driving towards something, not doing something just to 'fix a problem' or move away from a negative situation.

- The 'what' becomes intensely focused and you can make better decisions.

- You and your team member are more likely to be motivated by the 'why' and the results it can give you. These are often more motivational than the practicalities of the 'what'.

- You will have a clearer picture of what success looks/feels/sounds like for you so will recognise it when you get there.

- It makes objectives even SMARTer.

- You can use outcomes to give greater autonomy to others – you can tell them what they need to achieve, not how to achieve it. The only caveat here is that people with a lack of experience or knowledge may need extra support – but even here, outcomes are much more motivating than instructions.

So, when planning for maximum effectiveness for you and your team:

1. Understand your desired outcomes

What ultimate outcome are you trying to achieve? Don't be afraid of starting a briefing meeting, with *"what are we trying to achieve by the end of this meeting?" "What's the most useful outcome from this meeting?"*

2. Only now start to consider HOW you might you achieve them.

What works now, what could be better? Are there different means to achieving the ultimate end goal?

3. Revise your plan

Now get rid of anything in your plan or on

your to do list that does not contribute to your desired outcomes. Get focused.

All too often, people start with the 'how' but time spent on Step 1 is invaluable.

Let me give you an example.

As a manager, I might ask Fred to attend a training course called "Winning Business". This, however, is not the outcome (neither is it a SMART objective).

If we were to turn this into an outcome we would use our telescope to look to the future.

What is it we are trying to achieve for the future?

It may be:

- Develop and inspire Fred.

- Win more business.

- Provide Fred with some CPD hours.

- Turn Fred into Sales Man Extraordinaire.

As you can see there are a number of outcomes that are all possible from sending Fred on a course.

Suddenly, two things become clear:

Firstly, depending on the outcome you want, the sales training may or may not be worth spending time and money on.

Secondly, Fred's objective can be made more empowering for him (i.e. give him more autonomy over how he does this) and more impactful the business if it is outcome-driven.

Let's assume the outcome you really want is for Fred to win more business. His SMART, outcome-driven objective may now read:

"Generate 5 new fee-paying clients of over £20,000 value each for our team, within the next 12 months."

The course is now just part of the process to make this happen. Depending on Fred's level of capability and motivation, you may decide to add a bit more about the 'how' to his objective.

"To support you in this, we will fund your place on the 'Winning Business' course in January. You should be prepared to bring back the learning from the course to the team, so they can support you in your goal. You do not have to win all the clients alone but should use the course to make it happen within our team."

Driving to outcomes

There is only one question you really need to ask in order to start to get used to managing to outcomes and that is, 'Why?'

Keep asking yourself 'why are we doing this?' until you are happy that you have the right level of outcome to manage to.

Coffee break highlights

o As a manager, 'turning your telescope around' to understand the end goal is a powerful metaphor.

o What you do and the way you do it should be influenced by the outcome you are trying to achieve.

o Thinking about outcomes can help you focus on the right things and eliminate tasks that are superfluous.

o Keep asking 'why are we doing this?' until you get an answer that you are happy with. Then work backwards determine what you need to do to get there.

o You can start this approach in a small way by asking "what outcome do we want from this meeting?" More of this in the next Chapter.

Chapter 8

Make meetings count

I am sure most of us have been to meetings in our life where we have a felt a duty just to turn up and be there. We may even check the time whilst we are there and drift off, thinking about what's for tea.

Inevitably, your team will be influenced by your attitude towards meetings and your behaviour in them. And you really don't want to be a manager who has everyone in your team thinking it's enough to turn up.

If you start to master the skill of managing to outcomes, making meetings count will become a lot easier, but as they are a big part of work today (whether they happen face to face, on a call or Skype etc.), I wanted to dedicate a short chapter to them specifically.

When thinking about meetings and your team, the first question to ask yourself is "Why are we having a meeting?" Often, I find that people have been told they *should* have regularly, monthly meetings as these are the norm and, if they have taken over from a predecessor, often the first time manager will simply copy the old format.

You may well want to do this for your first

meeting, or perhaps two meetings, but I would invite you to very quickly review the purpose of the team meeting. Articulate, in one or two bullet points why it exists.

Common reasons will be to:

- Get together as a team socially and build relationships.

- Talk about the direction of the team or the business.

- Raise key project or client issues you are facing.

- Highlight any risks you face.

- Discuss sales, pipeline and conversion.

- Air any concerns.

- Celebrate success.

- Share knowledge and expertise.

- Inspire, engage and motivate.

There will be others specific to your organisation.

In the 80s and 90s, a big purpose of getting the

team together was to download information and in many organisations, I see this still being the focus – where people have not taken a step back and thought about the purpose and then, most importantly, thought about how it might be achieved differently and more effectively.

Getting people together in a room to tell them stuff or 'provide an update' is not always necessary (and often extremely dull unless it applies to everyone in the room) as you can use other mediums to make this happen – Skype, Discussion Forums, Pre-issue of documents, Webinars, Newsfeeds etc.

So, start by asking why. Then, once you have this firmly in your mind, ask your team what they think. What do they want from a team meeting? You need to know and to be able to have a robust response to the "What's in it for me?" question.

- Would they really value discussing the finer details of Bob's projects because they are on a similar project and really want to know how he solved some of the problems?

- Would they value social time and getting to know one another more informally afterwards?

- Do they need to listen to Rita's issue with a difficult client so they can ask her good questions to bring a fresh perspective and help her move forward?

Once you know what they want and need, you can then focus on how you can make it happen.

Things to ask are:

- Do we actually need to have a meeting or is another method of sharing information more appropriate? E.g. send your team a quick video recording from your phone, email them a document, post up a note on the team's newsfeed.

- Would we get a better outcome if the team had a chance to review information ahead of the meeting?

- What time works best – do you want an end of the week review or a Monday energiser?

- What is the best way to deliver the messages you need to? I would challenge you to have a Power Point free meeting at least once if you don't do this already, and see how that changes your preparation and the meeting outcome.

- Ask yourself, "How can I make this something people look forward to?" This might be that you show a TED talk clip relevant to one of your team challenges, or just that you provide bacon baps for breakfast or a jam scone in the afternoon (don't knock it, we all know food bribery works!).

- Who else in the team can lead the meeting? You can create the 'space' but you do not have to own the floor, the flipchart and the pen.

- Can you use the meeting in any way to develop a team member? It's often a very supportive environment in which to develop presentation skills and confidence.

I once worked with a firm of architects who held their team meetings monthly over lunch. But lunch was prepared by the team. Every month, with use of the tiny office kitchen, a few members of the team were asked to plan, issue a menu upfront and work together to deliver lunch for the whole practice. A

fun element of competitiveness crept in and each month saw increasingly ambitious menus, lots of laughter and roles developing within the team which meant budding cooks learnt, whilst confident cooks led and supported others. People got to know each other and the team meeting was something people really looked forward to.

In another professional services firm, I have used Lego to help bring meetings alive. Using something abstract like Lego and asking a decent question can help people think more laterally and creatively and also create a memory, which is sometimes an important outcome.

For example, I may say "I have outlined the business strategy for the next year and our challenge for the next 30mins is to work together to create a model of what that might look like for our team". The outcome you are looking for is to use the tool (whatever it is) as a means to have the debate and discussion around the topic. It's not about the Lego or the shiny model you create, but the discussion around it.

Finally, think about how you will improve future meetings. Revisit the meeting purpose periodically and challenge whether it's still valuable and whether the format needs to be adjusted. Ask your team for feedback at the end of meetings. It's their meeting as much as it is yours. You can refer to the chapter on feedback for more support in this areas, but as a starter, just ask:

- Did we achieve what we set out to achieve?

- What worked well?

- What could we do differently next time?

Importantly, act on any feedback to make future meetings better.

Coffee break highlights

o Make your meetings count by initially asking why you are having them. What do you need a meeting for? What's the outcome? Do you need a meeting at all?

o Ask your team members what the most useful outcomes would be for them.

o Try to design a meeting that meets the outcomes and is also something people would look forward to.

o Use the meeting as an opportunity to develop other people in the team. Just because you own the meeting, you don't have to lead it all, or do all the preparation.

o Ask for feedback at the end of each meeting – and act on it.

Chapter 9

Manage the 'waiting to be tolds'

Let's imagine that, despite avidly following the guidance in this book so far, you still have some people in your team that are career coasters. This is not to say they actually underperform, but are happy to sail along at a steady pace 'bobbing along'.

These are the people I call 'waiting to be tolds' – the individuals who come along to a meeting with their manager asking what their next year might look like, where you think they might go next, what they 'should' do.

I am all for helping and supporting people but this section is really about having a conversation about the R-word:

Responsibility.

Years ago, I was pondering over a big life decision that I needed to make about my job and where I lived as a result. It was a hard decision – I asked friends their opinion, sought advice from family and, well, anyone who would listen to be honest. I think even a visiting dog had its ear bent one night (dogs, for the record, are great at listening but are pretty rubbish with answers). Finally, two months of prevarication and procrastination led me to a coffee with a good friend. His words were wise. "It does not matter how many people you ask; the decision is yours. No one cares as much about your job as you do. They are too busy worrying about their own life."

At first, I thought this was a bit harsh. People did care about me and my decision would impact on them too. On reflection though, I realised he did not mean that people did not care about me, just that my life was my life. It was my decision to make.

I tell this story because one of my own bugbears is people who want others to take responsibility for their career and I think his words **'no-one cares about your job as much as you do'** are powerful.

Depending on our own personal circumstances, many of us will be expecting to work in some form for about 40 years or more. Let's say, for 8hrs a day. 330+ days a year for 40 years. That's a lot of hours in our lives.

Why then, do I meet so many managers in our field that tell me that professional, qualified people, most of whom have been to college for years to qualify in their field, come into appraisal/career planning conversations with a blank sheet of paper, waiting to be told what to do with their career, or asking their manager "what courses do you think I should go on this year?"

As you have picked up this book, I am guessing you are not a 'waiting to be told'. But you may manage one – or more than one.

If you do, then here are some compelling reasons that you can use to encourage people to step up and take responsibility for their career.

Reason 1. As my wise friend says "no one cares as much about your career as you do." Not even the best manager in the world.

Reason 2. As I have said before, if you want to get on, make yourself as useful as you can to your line manager. Don't give them work to do. Entering a career conversation (which is about their career!) with a blank sheet of paper, gives you, as their manager, a job.

Reason 3. Advice passed on to me by a wise CEO. "If you want to be considered for an opportunity you have to have 'first thought status' – i.e. you are the first person someone thinks of when they see or hear of an opportunity. If you are a passenger in a career conversation, how will anyone, let alone your personal advocate (i.e. you as their line manager) know what sort of opportunities interest you with clients or in your own workplace?

Reason 4. Only you know what really motivates you. Good managers (that's you) will coach and guide and ask good questions to help, but it is not your responsibility to tell someone what they want from their work life; it's their responsibility to have given it thought.

 We are all constrained by 'inhibitors' at times – fear, procrastination, lack of confidence or self-belief etc. Even some of the most outwardly confident people I meet will often reveal something I would never have guessed upfront that can hold them back from taking action.

One of the most compelling exercises you can get someone to do to help them address their own inhibitors and 'step up' is to encourage them to:

- Ask themselves what they want to look back on their life and say about it.

- Consider what they might say about it right

now.

- Recognise the gap (if there is one) and make a personal plan to do something about it.

The important bit here is to encourage them to do it – you do not need to know the answers. The process is far more important than the individual telling you the answers.

The point is that by knowing the 'gap' before they walk into a career conversation, they can drive their own agenda as well as listen to what's needed by the business.

The outcome of knowing the gap can also drive someone to aim higher - it might mean making an uncomfortable phone call, or doing a job they don't like to achieve a longer term goal or taking a risk they would otherwise not take.

If you are a manager of a 'waiting to be told' you might like to have these thoughts in your back pocket and craft a career conversation with these in mind – decent questions, along with your own experience and advice, can help you understand what's beneath the 'waiting-to-be-told' surface.

And, like most management conversations, it's

knowing what is beneath the behaviour that often leads to the best conversations that drive performance.

Coffee break highlights

o If you are managing a 'waiting to be told' you need to help them to take responsibility for their career.

o Ask them where they want to be in the future, compared to where they are now and then support them in making their own plan to fill the gap.

o Encourage the team member to own their career and seek out opportunities for growth and development themselves.

o Try to understand what is beneath their behaviour to create a spring board for action – it may be capability, but it could equally be fear, nervousness or lack of confidence.

Chapter 10

Help future stars shine

As an experienced professional, often your role will involve sharing your knowledge with those less experienced than you.

This may mean helping someone formally with their professional exams or their degree, or simply supporting them in their development on day to day basis (e.g. a Graduate or Apprentice).

Time is precious and often the pressure of client work can mean that explaining something new to someone can be frustrating, hurried or done in a way which does not support their learning or getting something done fast – we end up just telling them the answer or, even worse, just doing something ourselves because it is quicker than explaining it to someone else.

Having recently worked with some young people just starting on their journey into a professional services career, here I set out how to share your knowledge in an effective way which means both you and the trainee get something positive from the process.

It's much more effective than just telling someone what to do and will result in a better outcome for you and them.

1. **Put yourself in their shoes.** Simply take a few moments to think about what they know already that you can build on. Do they know about the project but not the task or do they understand the task, but need more information about the project? What is their emotional state? This is often overlooked, but emotions play an important part in performance. How will they feel about the task – is it a welcome challenge? Will they be fearful of it? Is it an area they are interested in? How will you reassure them if you need to? Will you need to check what they have done before it is sent to a client? How might they feel about that?

2. **Give context.** Context is important as it empowers the other person to ask intelligent questions. This means they add more value to the process for you (they may well think of something you have not thought of, too) and invites them to think about the overall outcome, which is far more motivating that just being given a task to do. This is also an important part of motivating juniors in the infancy of their career – "I had to check prices all day", "I had to make sure stuff was filed properly on the system", "I had to take notes in

a meeting" are some of the woes I hear from those still developing. Giving context is really easy and makes all the difference so start your briefing with lines like:

- "It's really important we make sure this report is accurate before the bank sign off funding"

- "Your notes will go to the client as an accurate record of the meeting. Meeting notes can be used in a dispute, so a key skill is to take accurate notes that are clear years down the line."

In the case of note taking, having a follow up conversation where any technical phrases or acronyms are explained can be much more helpful to you and the trainee than an email exchange where you just edit the final version before issue.

This may mean more preparation time for you, but will mean that you are more likely to get a 'right first time' response once your briefing is done. You will need to prepare though.

3. **Don't use acronyms.** If I was to ask you to write down all the acronyms your organisation

uses on a day to day basis, I would wager that you could rattle off a fair few. From industry jargon to abbreviated client names, why complicate a briefing session when you don't have to? By all means mention them, but use the proper words first. *"Fred - we are working for ABC on Project Silver at their HQ in the UAE so please can you call the M&E guys over there and ask them about the BIM platform they are using as we need to brief the QS team in the UK"* does not an empowering briefing make. I have overheard these types of conversations and seen the look on poor Fred's face as he walks away not really knowing what he needs to do or why. Indeed, I have been Fred quite a few times in my career.

4. **Agree a deadline or mini-deadlines.** You may well have a deadline that you need something done by and, of course, this should be clear. However, it's also powerful to discuss this and ask questions such as "what do you need from me to do this effectively?" "Do you want to do some of it and check in with me before you do it all?" "What other help do you need?" For very junior members of staff, you might ask them to "Have a think about what I have asked you to do and come back to me

with your questions in X time." This gives them permission to ask questions. Agreeing mini-deadlines and check-in points can also help them learn to plan ahead.

5. **Encourage great questions.** Asking great questions is a powerful skill, so when you are checking in on what's being done, encourage your mentee to prepare some questions that may be beyond the immediate task. For most professions a question like "If the answer we have reached is not what the client wants to hear, how might we deal with it?" is a good starting point. This makes the task much more interesting to the junior, broadens the context and develops their personal skills alongside the task in hand.

Qualified and experienced professionals do seem to genuinely like to share their knowledge - perhaps it's because someone else sat down with us and taught us something once and we feel a moral duty to pass it on. Or, as some management writers would suggest, we are motivated by 'mastery' and so passing on our knowledge makes us feel good.

Watching someone else suddenly understand

something is a great feeling and, if you use the tips above, you are likely to get more from the process too.

Coffee break highlights

o Think about the broader context and how you can build in learning opportunities whenever you give a junior a task.

o Don't use acronyms.

o Agree deadlines and mini 'check-in' deadlines.

o Give them time to process information and come up with their own questions.

o Think about briefing them with the why and the what, not just the how.

Chapter 11

Time is precious

Many managers working in professional services struggle with just not having enough time. Often they are juggling the demands of clients or projects, alongside managing a team within their organisation. A client calls or there is an urgent issue to deal with and other things need to get re-prioritised quickly, or a long working week ensues, trying to fit everything in. Often I observe that it's the internal team that suffers as the client or project takes priority. Or, it's the things that are truly important to you and your well-being that suffers – your favourite hobby, exercise, eating well and time with family and friends.

Alas, I have no secrets to share that will allow you to conjure up more than 24 hours in your day, but I will share with you the things I have found to be the most useful in my career and the constant challenge to make the most of the time that I do have.

Firstly, when I feel I am sinking, one of the most useful phrases I have in my mind (said to me by a professional coach as a 'throw-away' remark, but one that has stuck with me) is:

"Accept that there is always more that can be done. All you can do is to aim to make wise choices".

Against this backdrop, for me, there are two levels at play when we talk about 'managing time'.

The first operates at the macro level of our lives and invites us to ask the question, "Am I fundamentally spending time (i.e. my life) on the things that matter to me, or that take me towards my own big goals?" For this level, you might want to visualise yourself piloting your personal life 'helicopter', hovering over a field which represents where you are right now in your life. As you climb higher and higher, the details fade away and you're left with the landscape of the more fundamental choices you have (changing jobs, living abroad, taking a sabbatical, moving home, starting a family, going for a promotion, starting a new career etc.) stretching out in front of you.

Use your 'helicopter' view to ask yourself if what you are spending time on in that moment is the right thing in the context of your life as a whole or, at the next level down, in your role as a manager.

The second level operates at the micro-level, where you are on the ground, in your current 'field', getting stuff done. This is where you make your day-to-day, hour-to-hour choices – walk the dog, write the report, clean your teeth, go to a meeting, buy dinner, run, watch TV, 'phone a client, read your e-mails, have a 1:1 with a team member. When you're 'on the ground', you have lots of details and options to weigh up to make the right decisions for right now but your visibility is limited to your current field.

In an ideal world, you would use your helicopter view the inform what you do on the ground to make sure you're heading in the right direction, at least most of the time.

One of the challenges I find with any time management advice is that many managers want to just know how to cram more stuff into their day.

Whilst having this ability might seem appealing, I often find that this is a symptom of someone forgetting about (or avoiding) their helicopter and just focus on getting stuff done. Without the clarity of goals and direction the helicopter provides, 'busyness' can become an individual's personal gauge of effectiveness and, to coin a phrase, they get 'lost in the weeds'.

Sometimes this can be because it is often harder to fathom what you see from the helicopter or, for some, it brings with it some big questions which are difficult (or maybe even painful) to answer.

The process outlined here aims to help you bring your helicopter and 'on the ground' views together. This is not always easy, but if you take one thing from this chapter, my advice would be to develop your helicopter vision.

1. **For a week, write down exactly how you spend your time.** From waking to sleeping. Include every change in activity and work and non-work activity. E.g. 6am. Got up, showered. Coffee, breakfast, in car by 7am. At station for 7.30am. Read papers on train for meeting at 8.30am... etc. Even the act of doing this will raise your awareness around how you spend your time.

2. **Consider the things that are really important to you to have or do in your life. This may take some time for you to work through.** That's fine – it's important to get right. It's important to give yourself the motivation to change and so be clear on what you want before you do any analysis of your current time. Do you want to be home by a certain time each night? Do you want to study a new skill? Do you want to be promoted? What are

your goals? Think about the team you have from your helicopter position too – what do they need from you? Where are you trying to take them?

3. **Once you are clear on your goals, it's time to look at how you spent Week 1.** This is about moving forward, not getting engrossed in where you are now. In particular think about:

   a. Identifying the time wasting stuff - what things in that week are just diverting you from your goals and could just be eliminated from your life? We all have them. TV, social media, or even doing work that, if you were honest, someone else could do or could be removed from your schedule altogether.

   b. Take some time to think about your helicopter view – are there short term things you are happy to do in the spirit of a longer term win? Does a move towards your goals mean a tiny change or a big shift like changing a big aspect of your life?

   c. Ask yourself if you have been taking on the helicopter view for your team? When you were on the ground, did you cancel an a 1:1 catch up with a team member because you were busy, but now, in your helicopter, realise that you have impacted on the team member's performance last week which may have an impact on your overall plan for the year.

4. **Plan your next week with a "when will I do" list.** Just like a revision plan for your exams, now is the time to plan next week. Turn your to-do list into a "when will I do" list. For all of us, there are things we have to do – and things we feel we should do because they are important to us or the team. These are the ones to put blocks of time in first with your new awareness of what is really important to you and the team. To help you plan your week, you can download a weekly planner from the Chaseville Consulting website at:

https://chaseville.co.uk/offers/when-will-i-do-planner/

The 'when will I do...' planner

Time slot	Monday	Tuesday	Wednesday	Thursday	Fr
06:00am					
07:00am					
08:00am					
09:00am					
10:00am					
11:00am					
Noon					
1:00pm					
2:00pm					
3:00pm					

5. **Review at the end of the week.** What really happened? Where is there still room for change? What went really well? What could have been better? If you are looking to change ingrained habits, that takes time. It can take about three months to change old habits, so bear this in mind. Just aim to do the different thing every day and don't make it into a big overwhelming change – think about tiny steps.

6. **Accept where you are right now.** Sometimes there are times when we are all just busy and snowed under and feel a bit overwhelmed. As well as using some of the tools above, acknowledging and accepting the things you

cannot (or do not really want to) do can reduce the pressure you put on yourself. If you are a parent, a carer or busy at work because you are working towards a much wanted promotion, recognise what this really means. Focus on the things you can and really want to change.

If you are suffering from overwhelm, I would urge you to speak to someone who can help you get back on track. This may be your partner, a peer, your line manager or even a professional coach.

Sometimes all it can take is someone to ask decent questions and help you review your list of priorities – other times you may need longer term support.

I remember once looking at despair at my 'to do' list – it spread over two pages of A4 and covered about sixty tasks. It was 2pm already and I'd done nothing that I had planned that day.

I walked into my line manager's office exhausted – it was the end of a long month working very long hours and I was tired and overwhelmed. In truth, in the moment, I could have easily walked out of the door never to return.

His response was to ask some questions and make observations like those below.

- Is anyone going to die if you don't do something on that list? (Don't take this to be flippant - this is not a flippant question if you work in construction and property).

- Mark on anything that must be done today to meet promises made to others.

- Can you move any of the deadlines?

- What are the consequences of each of those items if they never got done?

- Is there anyone in your team that can do any of those?

He also removed some things from my list – he had the power and authority to do this.

We ended up with four things that I had to do before I left that day and agreed on those.

He then passed me back my marked up list and said "Just do those. Then go home and don't come in tomorrow. Go swimming. Go running. Do what you like, but don't work and start next week afresh".

And that, in my view, is a great boss in action.

Coffee break highlights

- Accept that there is always more that can be done. All you can do is to aim to make wise choices.

- Explore the concept of the helicopter and 'on the ground' views. Knowing the view you are taking and how it is helping you (or not) is a very useful skill to develop.

- Plan with a 'when will I do it planner' to help you focus and prioritise.

- Constantly review your week and take small steps to improve each week.

Chapter 12

The easiest ways to give feedback

"Can I give you some feedback?"

For me, this is not a great way to start a feedback conversation – my heckles are raised even before the other person has said anything else.

"No thanks" are the words in my head, even if "Oh yes please, I cannot wait." are the ones that come out of my mouth, through a false smile.

This said, feedback is really important to driving performance upwards both in ourselves and within our teams and, if you have created an atmosphere of trust as per the early chapters in this book, then having open and honest feedback conversations in a bid to drive up performance individually and as a team can be super-powerful.

Before I give you some useful feedback models, there are a few of rules of feedback that I think are worth noting first.

- Feedback has to be specific enough to give the other person an idea of how they can improve.

- Tell the other person what the observable behaviour is. What do you actually see?

- After this, you may add how it made you feel.

This does not mean you have to be soft and fluffy, it just makes the feedback more useful and enhances its worth. E.g. "When you look down whilst I am talking to you, it makes me feel that you are not listening." It may well be that they absolutely are listening – but it's useful for them to know that looking down makes you believe they are not.

- You do not have to tell them what to do instead - often observations are enough.

- They must trust you enough for you to have a chance of influencing them. When did you ever listen to the opinion of someone whose opinion you did not trust?

- Before you open your mouth to speak, always consider the positive intent of your feedback. Think of the outcome you want before you start.

It should always aim to help someone and move them forward so formulating a 'positive intent' in your own mind is useful to gather your own thoughts.

Three feedback models new managers often find useful are set out below. These can be used in a group setting or with individuals.

1. **Stop, start & continue**

    Simply ask 'what can we stop doing, start doing and continue to do' and capture the results.

2. **What went well and what might we do differently next time?**

    Make sure you capture the good stuff with the question 'what went well?' before asking the next bit. Note that the word 'might' is deliberate as it opens the mind up to possibilities. If you replace 'might' with 'should' you can lead people to filter their ideas before they open their mouths.

3. **Three stars and a wish**

    This is a model I learnt from a 9-year-old, so earns its credibility from a primary school. I love it for its memorability and simplicity. It simply captures three good things and a 'wish' for something to be different going forward.

By far, the most useful feedback model I've seen

used with managers was one I gathered from working with actors at The Shakespeare Schools Festival in London. Actor Dominic Fitch demonstrated 'live' how three simple phases will drive up performance both during rehearsals with actors, and in teams in the corporate world.

What I love about these are that, as a manager, you do not give the answer – you simply make an observation that is specific enough for the other person to do something themselves. My own interpretation of this model, translated into the world of professional services, is below, but with full credit to Dominic's workshop.

"I notice..."

"I notice that when you were in the project meeting, you were looking down at your notepad for almost half of the time."

"I wonder what would happen if...."

"I wonder what would happen if you walked the floor and said hello to more people in our team every day."

"I like it when...."

"I like it when you update me on your to do list every week."

You can see how the specificity of the statements would help the receiver think "I will do more of X, less of Y and maybe try something new".

That's it. Really simple.

Coffee break highlights

o Start by considering your own positive intent. What outcome do you want as a result of giving the feedback?

o Be specific. 'Say what you see' and if you think it is appropriate, add how it makes you feel.

o For reviews of meetings, team performance, an activity or task useful models to use include 'stop, start, continue', 'what went well and what might we do differently?' and 'three stars and a wish'.

o If you are giving personal feedback useful lines to start with are 'I notice', 'I wonder what would happen if' and 'I like it when'.

o Role model how useful feedback can be by asking for and acting on it yourself.

Chapter 13

How are you doing?

Now is the time to reflect and understand your own areas of further development and your personal next steps. I've listed the areas we have focused on here, so you can consider where you are with each.

Of course, this is just the start of your management journey.

Remember that learning to be a manager is just like learning to be a professional all over again – it takes time, practice, mistakes and failures to learn from, and experience.

I truly hope that you keep this book in your back pocket during the first few months in your new role and find it a useful 'friend' to help you embrace the management challenge you have been given.

Here's a quick reminder of the journey we have been on together already. By now, you have:

- Identified your own web for success.

- Started to build new relationships based on a developing bedrock of trust.

- Had more conversations that matter.

- Understood what is expected of you.

- Set meaningful goals for your team.

- Started using outcomes to identify what you do and the way you do it.

- Started to support any 'waiting to be tolds' and future stars.

- Started giving constructive feedback.

This is just the beginning of your journey.

For more help and support, you can also follow Chaseville on Facebook at Be Great @ Work with Chaseville Consulting for everyday tips for the workplace, or to receive updates via email, sign up to our mailing list at:

https://chaseville.co.uk/signup-hiam/

References & Further Reading

This book represents the culmination of my own experience and the influence of significant books that have made a real difference to my thinking and approach. Here's a list of a few of my favourite books which have influenced my thinking and developed me as an individual and a manager which you may find of value.

Empowering Yourself – The Organisational Game Revealed, Harvey J Coleman ISBN-10: 1449080340 ISBN-13: 978-1449080341 (Includes the PIE model)

Managing the Professional Services Firm, David Maister, ISBN-10: 0743231562 ISBN-13: 978-0743231565

How to Win Friends and Influence People, Dale Carnegie, ISBN-10: 0091906814, ISBN-13: 978-0091906818

Eat That Frog – Get More of the Important Things Done Today, Brian Tracy. ISBN-10: 1444765426, ISBN-13: 978-1444765427

Drive – The Surprising Truth about What Motivates Us, Daniel Pink, ISBN-10: 184767769X, ISBN-13: 978-184767769

Start with Why – How Great Leaders Inspire Everyone to Take Action, Simon Sinek, ISBN-10: 0241958229, ISBN-13: 978-0241958223

The First 90 Days – Critical Success Factors for New Leaders at All Levels, Michael Watkins, ISBN-10: 1422188612, ISBN-13: 978-1422188613

The 7 Habits of Highly Effective People, Powerful Lessons in Personal Change, ISBN-10: 0684858398, ISBN-13: 978-0684858395

Printed in Great Britain
by Amazon